Crown Me

Life is a game of chess. We are to learn God's strategic moves in order to overcome him and win the Victor's Crown.

Written by: Birdella A. Tucker
Foreword by Jacob Biswell

Copyright © 2016 by Birdella A. Tucker
All rights reserved. This book or any portion thereof
may not be reproduced or used in any manner
whatsoever without the express written permission
of the publisher except for the use of brief
quotations in a book review.

All Scripture unless otherwise noted taken from KING JAMES
VERSION (KJV): KING JAMES VERSION, public domain.

Printed in the United States of America

First Printing, 2016

ISBN-13:
978-0692746912 (Birdella A. Tucker)

ISBN-10:
0692746919

www.pearlboxministries.com

birdietucker@hotmail.com

SPECIAL THANKS

<u>Traci Tucker & Mary Renteria</u>

Your years of encouragement and prayer support for me and the ministry are priceless

<u>George Tucker</u>

My husband and my friend.

I praise God for our many years of marriage

<u>Tom Tucker</u>

My son – thank you for your love and support

<u>Jacob Biswell</u>

Your time taken to format this book and partnering with me in getting the revelation out there is

Invaluable

Colin Weber, cover

FOREWORD

As a child, my absolute favorite game was that of checkers. I always looked forward to making it to the other side of the board to be "crowned" and getting to shout "King me!"

Having grown up under the tutelage of Birdella, I've lived out the rules that places in this book – knowing full well the inheritance and the purpose that belonged to me. For as long as I can remember, Birdella has instructed me in the way I should go. My prayer is that as you read the revelation that pours forth from her heart you too will be transformed and will excitedly proclaim, "Crown me!"

Jacob Biswell

Introduction

The Word Metanoia means to go beyond the person as we see ourselves as to the person God created us to be. In Hebrews 6, we are instructed not to lay the same foundation of repentance from dead works, but change into the maturity of saints into the image of Jesus Christ. This book is about changing ourselves by the Word of God and by overcoming the dictates of the flesh. As when a person playing checkers reaches the other side of the board is crowned, so those in life who enter into the resurrection of Jesus are transformed.

Man is to put all things under God's dominion and was crowned with God's glory and honor. This crowning is only after man is regenerated by the renewal of his life through Jesus. In 2 Chronicles Solomon, the son of David, received the crown to rule from his father, King David. Solomon had prestige, wealth, position, and love from Israel. But, one thing he desired most of all, was to seek the Lord God before the tabernacle of the Lord (2 Chronicles 2:6-12).

6.   And Solomon went up thither to the brazen altar before the Lord, which was at the tabernacle of the congregation, and offered a thousand burnt offerings upon it.

7.   In that night did God appear unto Solomon, and said unto him, Ask what I shall give thee.

8.   And Solomon said unto God, Thou hast showed great mercy unto David my father, and hast made me to reign in his stead.

9.   Now, O Lord God, let thy promise unto David my father be established: for thou hast made me king over a people like the dust of the earth in multitude.

10. Give me now wisdom and knowledge, that I may go out and come in before this people: for who can judge this thy people, that is so great?

11. And God said to Solomon, Because this was in thine heart, and thou hast not asked riches, wealth, or honour, nor the life of thine enemies, neither yet hast asked long life; but hast asked wisdom and knowledge for thyself, that thou mayest judge my people, over whom I have made thee king:

12. Wisdom and knowledge is granted unto thee; and I will give thee riches, and wealth, and honour, such as none of the kings have had that have been before thee, neither shall there any after thee have the like.

Solomon became heir to his father's throne, but now, he says to God, "Crown Me!" Solomon was making the exchange, one crown for another crown. It was not enough to be established in this earth, he wanted a heavenly crown that can only come through metanoia, change from the natural to the eternal.

The game begins when the first player steps into one of the squares of the covenant. The enemy counters the play. Satan's desire is to either keep us from knowing our inheritance, or to keep us from obtaining it. He confronts each move we make with lies and wickedness. The goal of the game is for man to cross over the playing field to the opposite side and say, "Crown Me." Now, the playing field has changed. Man confronts the enemy not as man, but as king, not just any king, but as one who has been reborn into the image of Jesus, and who knows his inheritance and authority over Satan.

Before we can start any encounter with the enemy, we need to know the rules of the game and see who we are in Christ.

Birdella A. Tucker

RULE 1
The Mount of Transfiguration

After six days Jesus taketh Peter, James, and John his brother, and bringeth them up into a high mountain apart. (Matthew 17:1)

Notice, after six days Jesus takes three of His disciples up to a high place. This high place is symbolic of the presence of God. In the Book of Genesis, we read that God worked six days, called the work good, then created a seventh day, a day of rest. This "rest" is a place in the Son, who is the Rest.

In Psalm 62:5 David says, "Yes, my soul, finds rest in God."

Our soul labors on earth to do a work to bringing the Eternal Kingdom of God in heaven to earth. Once accomplished, we present that work to the Father in the Son by the Holy Spirit. When we have finished the assignment given to us by our Father, and we present it back to Him, <u>that work is crowned.</u> We have overcome the attacks against our soul. The crowning of the work tells us that metanoia, (change in one's way of life from penitence or spiritual conversion), has taken place.

Peter, James, and John saw the finished work of Jesus in the spirit before it took place. They experienced a "quantum" resurrection or a transportation into the future called translation. Habakkuk 2:1-3 says, "I will stand upon my watch, and set me upon the tower, and will watch to see what he will say unto me, and what I shall answer when I am reproved. And the Lord answered me, and said, Write the vision, and make it plain upon tables, that he may run that readeth it. For the vision is yet for an appointed time, but at the end it shall speak, and not lie: though it tarry, wait for it."

Jesus was giving the disciples a vision of the resurrection life after His death, and that those who are in Him through belief in acceptance of His salvation, will enter. Being alive in Jesus was their future. It is also rule number one. Without entering into Jesus first, any attempt to confront Satan will fail.

The disciples also saw Moses and Elias talking with Jesus confirming that the dead in Christ live in the future with Jesus. While they were pondering what was happening, a voice came out of a cloud, which said, "This is my beloved Son, in whom I am well pleased; hear ye him." According to Scofield, the transfiguration scene contains, in miniature, all the elements of the future kingdom in manifestation:

(1)   The Lord, not in humiliation, but in glory.

(2)   Moses glorified, representative of the redeemed who have passed through the death into the kingdom.

(3)   Elijah, glorified, representative of the redeemed who have entered the kingdom by translation.

(4)   Peter, James, and John, not glorified, representatives (for the moment) of Israel in the future kingdom.

(5)   The multitude at the foot of the mountain representative of the nations who are to be brought into the kingdom after it is established over Israel.

When the cycle of the assignment returns to the Father, the work is glorified. The person who overcomes is glorified or recognized as having entered into the presence of the Father. Our land receives glory and increase. And, others become established in the truth you have learned.

RULE 2
The Work of the Lord

We can only do what Jesus did.

1. We have heard with our ears, O God, our fathers have told us, what work thou didst in their days, in the times of old.

2. How thou didst drive out the heathen with thy hand, and plantedst them; how thou didst afflict the people, and cast them out.

3. For they got not the land in possession by their own sword, neither did their own arm save them: but thy right hand, and thine arm, and the light of thy countenance, because thou hadst a favour unto them.

4. Thou art my King, O God: command deliverances for us.
    (Psalm 44:1-4)

God the Father completed all the work that we are to accomplish in the first six days of creation, then rested, or put that work in Jesus. When we become believers of Jesus, the work that is in Him is to manifest in us as we experience the transformation in Jesus. If we trust in our own strength to do a work for God, we fail in our assignment.

"No one knows this work except the spirit of man in himself and is known by the Spirit of God" (I Corinthians 2:11).

We have received this assignment, not to hide it in our earthen vessel, but to reveal it so that God will say of us,
"This is my beloved . . . in whom I am well pleased."

The natural man does not see or understand this work. Only the Spirit in man can discern or reveal this work to us. Once we receive an assignment, we are to deal with that area of our soul that is un-renewed. Then, we are to bring this assignment to the cross and allow all of our strength and ability to perform this work crucified in Jesus. Then, and only then, will the Holy Spirit raise up the work in Himself so that change has occurred in our character and nature, "metanoia", has manifested.

The person who does this is "Buried with him in baptism, wherein also ye are risen with him through the faith of the operation of God, who hath raised him from the dead" (Colossians 2:12).

"But if the Spirit of him that raised up Jesus from the dead dwell in you, he that raised up Christ from the dead shall also quicken your mortal bodies by his Spirit that dwelleth in you" (Romans 8:11).

Referring back to the "checkerboard" game, we are only crowned once we pass through the attacks by bringing our reaction to the attacks to be buried in Christ. Only after death occurs will the Holy Spirit raise us up to be transformed into the image of Jesus with His name and authority to confront the adversary. Any goal that we attempt to reach in our own strength will fail. Consequently, we will not be crowned as we did not overcome by the Blood of Jesus. Result—no metanoia, no transformation. Paul encourages us in Hebrews 6:

1. Therefore leaving the principles of the doctrine of Christ, let us go on unto perfection; not laying again the foundation of repentance from dead works, and
   of faith toward God,

2. Of the doctrine of baptisms, and of laying on of hands, and of resurrection of the dead, and of eternal judgment.

3. And this will we do, if God permit.

Jesus is the King of Kings. He has called us to be kings on earth to manifest His glory and to speak in all power and authority given to us in His name. While in the battle, we need to see our future deliverance and position in Him. There is always a battle before the resurrection. If we fight this battle in our strength, we postpone the glory that is to be given to the Father and His Words of sonship. The future we are to have is upon the foundation of covenant relationship. Not all attacks are because we have sinned, but because of the plan, we are to be changed into His image. We must not forget what Jesus has done for us as seen in Isaiah 53:3-5

3.   He is despised and rejected of men; a man of sorrows, and acquainted with grief and we hid as it were our faces from him; he was despised, and we esteemed him not.

4.   Surely, he hath born our griefs, and carried our sorrows: yet we did esteem him stricken smitten of God, and afflicted.

5.   But he was wounded for our transgressions; he was bruised for our iniquities: the chastisement of our peace was upon him; and with his stripes, we are healed.

He was bruised, He was stricken, He was killed, (for us). Now, Lord, redeem us from the enemy who is trying to kill us and to keep us from being transformed into the image of Jesus. We have to know that the enemy is coming against the Christ in us to destroy Him. And, of course, he thinks that if he kills us, he destroys Jesus.

Psalm 9:

3.   When mine enemies are turned back, they shall fall and perish at thy presence.

4.   For thou hast maintained my right and my cause; thou satest in the throne judging right.

5.   Thou hast rebuked the heathen, thou hast destroyed the wicked, thou hast put out their name for ever and ever.

6.   But the Lord shall endure forever: he hath prepared his throne for judgment.

8. And he shall judge the world in righteousness, he shall minister judgment to the people in uprightness.

Years ago, there was a slogan, "What would Jesus do?" We have apparently forgotten to ask this question in our soul. How quickly, when oppression or persecution arises for the Words sake that we want to either fight outwardly or turn to bitterness within our soul. A good example of this came to me in my anger against someone steeling hay from my son. Tom raises alfalfa to sell, not for someone to steal his hay. However, after each harvest time when the bales of hay are stacked, someone sneaks in to steal the hay. My attitude has been, "Go get them, God!" or some other remark in vengeance. After three years of bitterness and seeing no relief from the thief, God gave me the following scripture to teach me a lesson from Habakkuk 1:2-5.

2.   O Lord, how long shall I cry, and thou wilt not hear! Even cry out unto thee of violence, and thou wilt not save!

3.   Why dost thou show me iniquity, and cause me to behold grievance? For spoiling and violence are before me: and there are that raise up strife and contention.

4.   Therefore the law is slacked, and judgment doth never go forth: for the wicked doth compass about the righteous; therefore wrong judgment proceedeth."

5.   Behold ye among the heathen and regard, and wonder marvelously: for I will work a work in our days, which ye will not believe, though it be told you.

6.   For, lo, I raise up the Chaldeans, that bitter and hasty nation, which shall march through the breadth of the land, to possess the dwelling places that are not theirs.

I saw that God would raise up the Chaldeans. The Chaldeans were a bitter and hasty people. As I prayed, I saw by the spirit that God called Abraham out of the land of the Chaldeans. I am in the loins of Abraham. If God called Abraham out of bitterness and of being hasty, then He called me out. I saw a vision of my translation, out of one place and into a new place, a place of blessings in Abraham. As I continued seeking God, I understood that I was wallowing in self-pity for what was happening to my son. I began to understand. That which confronted me was because there was a spirit of bitterness in me and in my land. It was like a checker piece hindering my advancement to the crown. Once I saw who I am to be in Jesus, (the transformation) I renounced and repented for the spirit of bitterness. Then, I was able to pray for the person or persons who were stealing hay to be saved from that, which bound them to Satan. I heard instructions, go to John 16 and read it. The very first words that are written are, "These things have I spoken unto you, that ye should not be offended." Too late. I was already offended. But, as I continued to read in verse 5, "But now I go my way to him that sent me; . . . verse 7, It is expedient for you that I go away: for if I go not away, the Comforter will not come unto you, but if I depart, I will send him unto you. And when he is come, he will reprove the world of sin, and of righteousness, and of judgment."

My mind went back to the story of the transfiguration. Jesus had to leave the natural world to return to the Father. He would be with us in our struggles and fears through the Comforter, the Holy Spirit. The answer I needed regarding this situation was placed in me during creation. It is my job to call upon the Holy Spirit to reveal something to me so that I could judge righteously by the Spirit and not by my flesh. As I consulted Him, He gave me a dream that revealed an iniquity in me called "slave mentality". Under slave mentality, or under a poverty spirit, I would want something for nothing because I didn't have the faith that Jesus would supply all of my needs. The Holy Spirit showed me that a thief is under this same spirit. He believes the only way he can obtain something is by stealing it. Neither they nor I knew the power to obtain my needs met by the Word of God.

We were created to be vessels in which living waters flow to those living in dry places. Those in bitterness do not inherit the joy they are to live in. I had to experience death to the bondage of bitterness and to the god of poverty mentality. I had to activate this living water that is in me because of Jesus. Under the Old Testament people had to thirst for the waters and then receive it not because they had money to purchase it, but because it was a free gift. Isaiah 55:1 says, "Ho, every one that thirsteth, come ye to the waters, and he that hath no money; come ye, buy, and eat; yea, come, buy wine and milk without money and without price. The wine is the covenant of blood through Jesus Christ. The milk represents the goodness of the Word of God that will satisfy. Jehovah Jira, one of the names of God, means God is my provider. As long as we look to doing a work within ourselves to provide for our needs, whether by having someone give something to us or by stealing it, the work is a work of the flesh and will not transform us into the image and power of Jesus.

The work reveals that we are not honoring God as the One who provides for us. Deut. 28:

47: Because thou servedst not the LORD thy God with joyfulness, and with gladness of heart, for the abundance of all things;

48: Therefore shalt thou serve thine enemies which the LORD shall send against thee, in hunger, and in thirst, and in nakedness, and in want of all things: and he shall put a yoke of iron upon thy neck, until he have destroyed thee.

"But" Isaiah 10:27 encourages us, saying, "And it shall come to pass in that day, that his burden shall be taken away from off thy shoulder, and his yoke from off thy neck, and the yoke shall be destroyed because of the anointing." This day that we are looking toward is hidden in the Scripture Isaiah 37. King Hezekiah is being tormented by threats of destruction (voices from the past). Hezekiah is told that he has no hope of survival. God will allow his destruction because of his former actions. "But" Hezekiah prays to God and humbles himself to give God the honor of seeking His face.

6.   Thus saith the LORD, Be not afraid of the words that thou hast heard, wherewith the servants of the king of Assyria have blasphemed me.

(We blaspheme God when we do not speak of who He is. He is a forgiving God. He is a God of forgiveness. He is a God who loves His children and desires them to turn to Him and away from the works of their own hands).

7.   Behold, I will send a blast upon him, and he shall hear a rumor, and return to his own land; and I will cause him to fall by the sword in his own land.

15.   And Hezekiah prayed unto the LORD, saying,

16.   O LORD of hosts, God of Israel, that dwellest between the cherubims, thou art the God, even thou alone, of all the kingdoms of the earth:

17.   Incline thine ear, O LORD, and hear; open thine eyes, O LORD, and see: and hear all the words of Sennacherib, which hath sent to reproach the living God.

Because Hezekiah humbling himself before the LORD, God sent help to stop the thief from stealing and killing.

Assyria represents our iniquities. There will come a time in which our responses to threats rise out of a spirit of bitterness. In Luke 9 Jesus exposes the iniquities of his disciples. First, in verse 46, Jesus perceives that His disciples are reasoning among them, which of them should be greatest. In order to teach them a truth, He brings a child into the midst and says,

48. Whosoever shall receive this child in my name receiveth me: and whosoever shall receive me receiveth him that sent me: for he that is least among you all, the same shall be great.

While the lesson of receiving Jesus is hot on their mind, they respond to Samaritans who did not receive Jesus who was about to enter their land.

54.   And when his disciples James and John saw this, they said, Lord, wilt thou that we command fire to come down from heaven, and consume them, even as Elias did?

55.   But he turned, and rebuked them, and said, Ye know not what manner of spirit ye are of.

When we consider our flesh to satisfy our needs or to promote us, we open a door for us to allow another spirit to control us. Jesus comes not to destroy men's lives, but to save. If our attitude is not to save someone, then we are of another spirit. If our attitude is feeling that God has not given us that which we desire, then we are of another spirit. Ephesians 1:3 says, God has already blessed us with all spiritual blessings in heavenly places. All these are in us who are in Christ. Our job is not to look at what we do not have, but look to the One who has given everything to us and ask Him how to make a spiritual withdraw from our heavenly account to crown us with it, on earth as we are crowned in heaven.

RULE 3
We have to be planted into His likeness by His death

Bitterness is not something we see in Jesus. Therefore, if I see it in me, I have to confess it as sin, repent for the spirit of bitterness, bind it to the altar to be crucified in Christ (allow bitterness to die in me), then experience the resurrected image of Jesus, the compassion of Jesus to forgive the thief on the cross.

Bitterness is a seed. Unless I bury it in Christ, I will not be able to jump the checker (overcome the attack) and take the enemy captive. Just as the checker piece is removed from the playing board when I do this, so bitterness is removed from my heart.

Recently I learned that in the Book of Esther, the name of Haman (God's enemy), is mentioned 54 times. However, the name of Esther is also named 54 times. For every move of Haman, God had a counter move until Haman was destroyed. God promises that the evil will not be more powerful than our defense in Jesus. I also learned that the spirit of Haman represented an antagonistic spirit that comes against our covenant. One of the outstanding promises in Esther is this:

God can re-write our history and turn things around by giving us power and permission to destroy our enemies and to overcome them when under attack.

Just as Jesus walked through the brook Kidron (Cedron), so will we on our journey to the other side in order to be crowned. The brook Kidron is a place in which the winter torrents flow through the Valley of Jehoshaphat (the valley of vision) or the valley of Judgment as some say. It lies on the eastern side of Jerusalem, between the city and the Mount of Olives. David crossed this brook bare-foot and weeping, when fleeing from Absalom (2 Samuel 15:23), (15:30), and it was frequently crossed by our Lord in his journeying to and fro (John 18).

1.   When Jesus had spoken these words, he went forth with his disciples over the brook Cedron, where was a garden, into which he entered, and his disciples.

2.   And Judas also, which betrayed him, knew the place: for Jesus ofttimes resorted thither with his disciples.

The definition of Kidron means making black, or obscure maybe because the torrent water was black in color. There are times on the checkerboard when life seems black and obscure. The visions we see are from the dark side of our iniquities that flood our thoughts and emotions. The torrent of accusations against us in our thinking are so strong we have a hard time seeing the vision of our being heirs to the Kings and joint heirs to Jesus. Instead of love flowing through us, darkness seems to have power to take us away from God's presence. These times seem so hard. As we press through them, focusing on God's plan for our lives, we come out to a place in which God will honor us (John 12:).

26.   If any man serve me, let him follow me; and where I am, there shall also my servant be: if any man serve me, him will my Father honor.

27.   Now is my soul troubled; and what shall I say? Father, save me from this hour: but for this cause came I unto this hour.

No one likes to have his soul troubled, let alone feel the accusations of the enemy as a black torrent of water beating against his very soul. However, for this cause we come to glorify the Father. Our Father is glorified when we repent for the iniquities within and allow them to be crucified with Jesus Christ. On one occasion, I felt so estranged from God that I wanted to run and hide from everyone. I felt I was separated from God's joy and could since the darkness of my soul. As I turned to the Holy Spirit, asking Him to guide me through this valley of darkness, I was determined to know my iniquity. Because I was sincere, I was shown that I had allowed a spirit of false obligation to enter. I would take on responsibilities that God had not given to me. Because of this, relationships became darkened. Instead of love flowing from me to them, I would ignore them and allow my once good relationship to be abandoned.

Darkness has a way of bringing forth either truth or lies. I call this place 6666.

1.   Exodus 6

It is time to leave (your flesh). I will bring you out of your burdens. I will bring you into your land. Speak unto Pharaoh (your flesh) all that I say unto you. Moses was instructed to tell the people to prepare to leave Egypt. We, like Israel, are to prepare to leave our flesh. We are to plow up the ground of our earthen vessel through repentance. The plowing stirs up the flesh and turns things around. Worms are exposed for the birds of the air (evil spirits of wickedness) to a feast. In Psalm 17 David cries out to God in prayer to protect him from the spirit of wickedness. He speaks to his vessel that he will not transgress either by word or deed. He asks for help to be kept as the apple of God's eye and cover him with God's wings of protection. He feels the spirit of oppression of the evil voices tempting him to criticize or act proudly. He then speaks prophetically concerning the rewards given to man. The rewards will either be that of the world (worldly) for those who justify themselves, and the eternal rewards of those who have passed through this temptation to draw upon God.

2.   Isaiah 6

In the year that king Uzziah died (your flesh), you will see God's glory. He will remove your iniquities for which you are ashamed. These are the things that held you in bondage to your carnal nature. The preparation spoken about in Exodus is the turning of your flesh over to the cross. At this time, as Satan has permission to eat our flesh, the worms come to the surface (attitudes) and evil spirits come to attack these. You will feel the oppressive spirits, but, like Jesus, if you press through this dark time in your life and pray as Jesus prayed in the Garden of Gethsemane, you will fulfill God's plan for your life. You now have two visions; one of His glory, and another one of your iniquities. You have a choice. You will receive either who you are as the new creation and move on with God, or you will return to the bondage of the flesh. If you repent and receive yourself as His heir, you will have life in you to pray for others. This reveals the crown of God's authority as heir. If not, you will return to your old ways not having power to save others.

3. Revelation 6

The iniquity that we deal with was once hidden in our subconscious. Jesus, the Lamb, has to open the seal for us to see. Revelation 6 confirms what Isaiah says, in that something comes at the time of awakening. However, in this chapter we see that there are a people who refuse to repent for the iniquities shown. Instead of having a voice of life to speak to others, they use their voice to try to protect their flesh and curse God.

If we judge ourselves strength will be given to us to establish something according to God's plan. Psalm 99:4 "The king's strength also loveth judgment; thou dost establish equity, thou executest judgment and righteousness in Jacob." God is a God of righteous judgment and righteousness. When we judge ourselves, we represent Him for who He is.

Each one of us are righteous in our own eyes and our sense of equity is far from the Lords. Example: The story of a householder hiring workers in Matthew 20. In the morning, the householder finds a worker and hires him for a penny a day. Later that day he finds another and hires him for a penny for the day. At the end of the day, he finds another worker and hires him for a penny for the day.

8.   So when even was come, the lord of the vineyard saith unto his steward, Call the labourers, and give them their hire, beginning from the last unto the first.
9.   And when they came that were hired about the eleventh hour, they received every man a penny.

10.   But when the first came, they supposed that they should have received more; and they likewise received every man a penny.

11.   And when they had received it, they murmured against the goodman of the house,

12.   Saying, These last have wrought but one hour, and thou hast made them equal unto us, which have borne the burden and heat of the day.

13.   But he answered one of them, and said, Friend, I do thee no wrong: didst not thou agree with me for a penny?

14.   Take that is thine, and go thy way: I will give unto this last, even as unto thee.

I used to hate this parable, for "my" sense of equality and righteousness was not the same as Jesus'. For me to have the righteousness and equity of God, I would have to pass my soul through the brook Kidron and let it experience the blackness of my sinful flesh. With the hope of who I am in Jesus, I had the strength for the journey.

4. John 6: The Works of God

For I come down from heaven, not to do mine own will, but the will of him that sent me. And this is the Father's will which seeth the Son, and believeth on him, may have everlasting life: and I will raise him up at the last day (verses 38-40). Until we eat of the life of Jesus, we will not be able to do the works of God. Our works will be after the spirit of Babylon which is to self-seeking.

"Let not your heart be troubled. The water that was troubled once a year at the pool of Bethesda brought healing to the first person who would step into the water. In John 12:27 I announced; "Now My soul is troubled." Just as the Israelites had to step into the Red Sea when their hearts were troubled, so must you when you feel the troubling of My soul in you. I am Living Water. I am the Red Sea. As you step into Me at this time you will be healed from the things that which trouble you." (Word given May 17, 2016)

In Ephesians 1:10 Paul tells us that there is a time in which the plans of God in heaven and the plans of God in our earthen vessel reach a fullness of time, an appointed time, to be

revealed on earth. The fullness of time is when we receive our inheritance (crown) as kings and priests unto God. When we are crowned, God receives the glory. We were predestined before we were born to be crowned. God's plan is "put into effect when the times reach their fulfillment—to bring unity to all things in heaven and on earth under Christ" (NIV),
This unity is between our spirit, soul, and body. Romans 8:

26.   Likewise, the Spirit also helpeth our infirmities: for we know not what we should pray for as we ought: but the Spirit itself maketh intercession for us with groanings which cannot be uttered.

27.   And he that searcheth the hearts knoweth what is the mind of the Spirit, because he maketh intercession for the saints according to the will of God.

28.   And we know that all things work together for good to them that love God, to them who are the called according to his purpose.

We will feel the groanings inside. It indicates that there is something inside of us that needs to be liberated from the flesh nature so that our soul can rule after God's Spirit.

We were made heirs to the kingdom at salvation. We do not work to become the heir; we work to destroy the flesh that hinders our position as heir. Everything we need is inside of us in Christ Jesus. It is our job to draw out of Him this life. The other night I saw a grave uncovered. I saw the cement casket in which the wood casket with the dead body is placed, empty.

As I prayed to the Lord, I heard . . . the empty cement casket is a sign that resurrection life has taken place. Had I seen the dead body in the cement casket, I would have evidence that resurrection had not taken place. To me, this meant that my flesh, that which was buried in Christ, was raised by the Spirit to join Jesus at the right hand of Father God.

Jesus tells us in John 6 not to work for the bread that perishes, but for that which endures unto everlasting life. After Jesus fed the 5,000, He left to cross over to the other side of the lake. Many who ate the bread followed Him. However, Jesus confronted their reasons for following Him. If what we do does not produce eternal life, then we miss the true meaning of following Jesus. Our work stays as the dead body in the casket.

Rule 4
Our Inheritance, Rights to the tree of life.

We are to have life flow out of us to give life to others.

The tree of life began as a seed planted within a mortal body. This mortal body was born in sin with a sin consciousness that he would pass on to succeeding generations unless they turned to Jesus. Man, even though saved in his spirit, has a poverty mentality until he learns what the covenant given to him contains. The growth of man is in three stages, much like the three stages of pregnancy. In stage one we become pregnant with Jesus in our spirit. Our mind remains in bondage until it is renewed by the Spirit. The second stage is servanthood. Man, though saved, attempts to serve God by the rules of engagement only to become discouraged. The third stage is sonship. Now, this born-again believer serves God by taking his place as king over that which God has given to him to possess. This person overcame the voices of the enemy who tempted him to stay engaged in war without ever entering into Rest.

For each confrontation that a person overcomes in Christ, another generation will experience a blessing. God saw the sacrifice of His Son and counted it toward another generation.

"A seed shall serve him; it shall be accounted to the Lord for a generation" (Psalm 22:30).

The story of the "prodigal son" in Luke 15, is a wonderful picture of the crowning. "But the father said to his servants, Bring forth the best robe, and put it on him; and put a ring on his hand, and shoes on his feet: And bring hither the fatted calf, and kill it; and let us eat, and be merry: For this my son was dead, and is alive again; he was lost, and is found. And they began to be merry."

The son returned home to become a slave in his father's house. The father, however, wanted a son. The Father will not leave the servant's clothes on us. He will order them to be removed. Our Father is waiting for us to return to Him to be positioned at His right hand of authority in His Son. The Son has power to impart life. The new garments are robes of righteousness that bear the fruit of righteousness.
We have a right to eat from this tree of righteousness.

"He that hath an ear, let him hear what the Spirit saith unto the churches; To him that overcometh will I give to eat of the tree of life, which is in the midst of the paradise of God (Revelation 2:7).

"Hope deferred maketh the heart sick: but when the desire cometh, it is a tree of life" (Proverbs 13:12).

"And because ye are sons, God hath sent forth the Spirit of his Son into your hears, crying, Abba, Father" (Galatians 4:6).

Jesus is the source of righteousness. We are to receive our inheritance from Him

The word receive in the Greek is "Lambano" which means to accept as an owner who possess his inheritance regarding the thoughts and emotions in his soul. Acts 1:8 says, "But ye shall receive power, after that the Holy Ghost is come upon you: and ye shall be witnesses unto me both in Jerusalem, and in all Judea, and in Samaria, and unto the uttermost part of the earth.

When we experiencing a crowning from our thoughts and emotions, we are in position to allow the life-giving water of His Love to flow through our thoughts and emotions. God created us to express His image and to dwell in His likeness. Being crowned does not stop Satan from attacking. He wants our crown so he attacks our godly desires.

Satan's intent is to take our godly desires

There are godly desires that Satan wants to take from us, and then there are desires that are merged with evil. David knew that unless his desires were perfect, as in Psalm 138, his desires would open a door for evil. When we keep our desires within our soul, (mind and emotions) instead of committing them to the Lord, these once good desires begin to cast a shadow of darkness on that which we desired and begin to listen to evil council.

Ps 138:2 says, " I will worship toward Your holy temple, and praise Your name for Your loving-kindness and for Your truth and faithfulness, for You have exalted above all else Your name and Your word, and You have magnified Your word above all Your name!"

Unless we know God's Word and exalt it above all else by submitting to it, we will be tempted to exalt our desires above God thinking we are submitting to God. "For my people have committed two evils; they have forsaken me the fountain of living waters, and hewed them out cisterns, broken cisterns, that can hold no water" (Jeremiah 2:13).

A cistern is a container, like the mind or heart that holds something. We were created to hold the Living Water of God's Word in these areas.

Joshua 1:8 "This book of the law shall not depart out of your mouth, but you shall meditate on it day and night, that you may observe and do according to all that is written in it, for then you shall make your way prosperous, and then you shall deal wisely and have good success."

James 1:8 Man of two minds.
a. One is unreliable, (carnal, unrenewed mind), hesitates to obey God; and unstable as he looks to what he thinks and feels-what will make him rich in his own eyes (happy, complete, etc.).

b.   1:24 observes himself, what pleases himself—has nothing to give to lay at God's feet. It is self-pleasing, taking the glory for the way he feels to himself.
  Mind of Christ, looks to what pleases God to bring Him glory- looks to the crown of life in which he can lay at Jesus' feet.

c.   Being a true heir, this person receives the blessings of a son by rights of inheritance through the covenant of blood. (Death, burial, and resurrection). He gave his desires to Jesus

Eli's sons began to walk by the light of their own desires of lust. They followed in the same sin as their forefathers, Adam and Eve.

The word knew is the Hebrew word "yada" (#3045), means to know, learn, perceive, recognize, confess, be instructed, to declare, and to reveal. What we do is for the purpose of "Knowing—Yada" God (Genesis 3:7).

When we seek for knowledge and truth for our satisfaction to fill our desires, we are broken cisterns that cannot hold the life of the Father.

The (Torah) law of Moses was given to man to "Yada" God, Jesus, and the Holy Spirit.

St. John 1:17 says, "For the law was given through Moses; grace and truth were realized through Jesus Christ." As long as man is under the control of his lower nature, his knowledge is that of the laws of do's and don'ts. It is something man could not live by as there was no life in it.

After Job was tested, he said, He knew (Yada) God. He learned submission by what he suffered only to recognize and confess Jesus as Lord and Savior of his spirit, soul, mind, emotions, and body.

Cain experienced the power of having desires according to his lower nature. The word desire in this text is #8669 in Strong's meaning longing, craving as a man for a woman or a woman for a man or beast to devour. God was saying evil crouches at every desire that we have which is not perfect toward God (Genesis 4:7).

False desires weaken our crown

Anger and fear act as a hindrance to keep us from entering into our promises

In Revelation 5:3-4 John weeps because there appears to be a hindrance to opening and reading the book which he saw. The Maxwell Leadership Bible speaks about the Law of the lid in I Samuel 17:24-40. A lid is something which comes to hinder our success like anger or fear, so that we do not rise above the hindrance. We have seen that man attempts to remove these hindrances and obtain his destiny by blaming others, refusing to forgive, sympathy, depression, aggression, and physical violence. But, when none of these tactics work, another law remains in force—the law of the lid. Just as the Lion of the tribe of Judah had to come and open the book, so God's anointed vessel has to be sent with His Word. The lid is something or someone who has come to defy the armies of Israel (or us).

In I Kings 20 we read about Ben-hadad king of Syria who, with his troops, besieged Samaria asking of Ahab, king of Israel, his silver, gold, and wives. Ahab consents to this request, but when Ben-hadad returns with another demand to search Ahab's house and "whatever is desirable in his eyes" he will take" (I Kings 20:6), Ahab resisted. In this scripture the word desirable is in Strong's and means that which is pleasant, beloved. Ahab draws the line. He realized that Ben-hadad wants to take away everything that brings him joy and happiness. This is what Satan is doing to us today. The name Ben-hadad means false god. Ben-hadad represents false desires. A false god comes to everything we trust in to satisfy our desires outside of Jesus Christ. Satan is not just after our physical possessions; he wants to take away that which brings pleasure to God in our spirit so that we will feel estranged from Him. Another story regarding failure to rise above evil passions is in the story of Ahab and Naboth's vineyard found in I Kings 21:

Now it came about after these things, that Naboth the Jezreelite had a vineyard which was in Jezreel beside the palace of Ahab king of Samaria. And Ahab spoke to Naboth, saying, "Give me your vineyard, that I may have it for a vegetable garden because it is close beside my house, and I will give you a better vineyard than it in its place; if you like, I will give you the price of it in money." But Naboth said to Ahab, "The Lord forbid me that I should give you the inheritance of my fathers." So Ahab came into his house sullen and vexed because of the word which Naboth the Jezreelite had spoken to him; for he said, "I will not give you the inheritance of my fathers." And he lay down on his bed and turned away his face and ate no food.

Ahab failed to rise above his greed which took him to a place of darkness because he didn't get his way. Darkness drew unwise counsel from his wife, Jezebel. She devised a plan to get Naboth's vineyard by deceit and lies. She wrote letters in Ahab's name and sealed it with his seal to the elders and the nobles living with Naboth in his city. She ordered them to plant two worthless men to accuse Naboth of cursing the king, which was punishable by death. As a result, Naboth was stoned to death and Ahab took his land because greed opened the door to a deeper darkness or evil. Greed was the valve, (opening, gate, door,) which allowed something to enter his heart. Jesus is the door to our heart. If we open up this door, (gate, portal) Jesus comes with His ways. If we open up the door to another desire in us that is under rebellion, then we open ourselves up to evil.

RULE 5

God created us to reproduce after His nature.

One of the fruits from the life of Jesus is this: He protects His people. We, in turn, are to be a protection for others when He asks us to. "There was a man called Oskar Schindler, a German industrialist, spy, and member of the Nazi Party who is credited with the saving of 1,200 Jews during the Holocaust. Schindler grew up with all the privileges money could buy. His exploits with women are a legend. Yet, God used him as His agent to save His people. Schindler hired Jews to work in his factory and set up a branch of the camp for 900 Jewish factory workers keeping them from being killed.

The Seed that Jesus placed in him was the seed of provision. Jesus feed 5,000 men, not counting the women and children, who were hungry and in need. Schindler, who did not know Jesus at the time, did the same. Oh, maybe he did not do it the same way, but with the same heart of God. God used him to feed His people and care for them.
 Corri Ten Boom is another example of bearing fruit after Jesus. "Corri was a Dutch Christian who, along with her father and other family members, helped many Jews. The family owned a

small jewelry store in a narrow house in the heart of the Jewish section of Amsterdam. There, in Amsterdam in that narrow street in the ghetto they met many wonderful Jewish people. They were allowed to participate in their Sabbaths and in their feasts. She was 48, unmarried and worked as a watchmaker in the shop that her grandfather had started in 1837. Her family were devoted members of the Dutch Reformed Church. Her father was a kind man who was friends with half of the city of Harlem. Her mother had been known for her kindness to others before her death from a stroke.

Corrie credits her father's example in inspiring her to help the Jews of Holland. She tells of an incident in which she asked a pastor who was visiting their home to help shield a mother and newborn infant. He replied, "No definitely not. We could lose our lives for that Jewish child." She went on to say, "Unseen by either of us, Father had appeared in the doorway. 'Give the child to me, Corrie,' he said. Father held the baby close, his white beard brushing its cheek, looking into the little face with eyes as blue and innocent as the baby's. 'You say we could lose our lives for this child. I would consider that the greatest honor that could come to
my family'" (Ten Boom, 1971, p. 99).

Corrie's involvement with the Dutch underground began with her acts of kindness in giving temporary shelter to her Jewish neighbors who were being driven out of their homes. She found places for them to stay in the Dutch countryside. Soon the word spread, and more and more people came to her home for shelter. As quickly as she would find places for them, more would arrive. She had a false wall constructed in her bedroom behind which people could hide.

After a year and a half, her home developed into the center of an underground ring that reached throughout Holland. Daily, dozens of reports, appeals, and people came in and out of their watch shop. Corrie found herself dealing with hundreds of stolen ration cards each month to feed the Jews that were hiding in underground homes all over Holland. She wondered how long this much activity and the seven Jews that they were hiding would remain a secret.

On February 28, 1944, a man came into their shop and asked Corrie to help him. He stated that he and his wife had been hiding Jews and that she had been arrested. He needed six hundred gilders to bribe a policeman for her freedom. Corrie promised to help. She found out later that he was a quisling, an informant that had worked with the Nazis from the first day of the occupation. He turned their family in to the Gestapo. Later that day, her home was raided, and Corrie and her family were arrested (their Jewish visitors made it to the secret room in time and later were able to escape to new quarters).

Corrie's father died within 10 days from illness, but Corrie and her older sister Betsie remained in a series of prisons and concentration camps, first in Holland and later in Germany. Although for many people, the concentration camp would have been the end of their work, for Corrie and Betsie the months they spent in Ravensbruck became "their finest hour." In her book, Corrie described how she struggled with and overcame the hate that she had for the man who betrayed her family and how she and Betsie gave comfort to other inmates.

Corrie describes a typical evening in which they would use their secreted Bible to hold worship services: "At first Betsie and I called these meetings with great timidity. But as night after night went by and no guard ever came near us, we grew bolder. So many now wanted to join us that we held a second service after evening roll call. . . (These) were services like no others, these times in Barracks 28. A single meeting night might include a recital of the Magnificat in Latin by a group of Roman Catholics, a whispered hymn by some Lutherans, and a sotto-voce chant by Easter Orthodox women. With each moment the crowd around us would swell, packing the nearby platforms, hanging over the edges, until the high structures groaned and swayed."

"At last, either Betsie or I would open the Bible. Because only the Hollanders could understand the Dutch text we would translate aloud in German. And then we would hear the life-giving words passed back along the aisles in French, Polish, Russian, Czech, and back into Dutch. They were little previews of heaven, these evenings beneath the light bulb" (Ten Boom 1971, p. 201).

Betsie, never strong in health, grew steadily weaker and died on December 16, 1944. Some of her last words to Corrie were, "...(we) must tell them what we have learned here. We must tell them that there is no pit so deep that He is not deeper still. They will listen to us, Corrie, because we have been here" (Ten Boom, 1971, p. 217).

Due to a clerical error, Corrie was released from Ravensbruck one week before all women her age was killed. She made her way back to Harlem, and tried for a while to go back to her profession of watchmaking, but found that she was no longer content doing that. She began traveling and telling the story of her family and what she and Betsie had learned in the concentration camp. Eventually, after the war was over, she was able to obtain a home for former inmates to come and heal from their experiences. And she continued to travel tirelessly over the world and tell to anyone who would listen the story of what she had learned. (Information taken from the internet).

The third person I have chosen to express the life of Jesus is Herbert Hoover, our 31st president of the United States. His actions were much like those mentioned above.

Hoover identified with the progressive wing of the Republican Party, supporting Theodore Roosevelt's third-party bid in 1912. World War I brought Hoover to prominence in American politics and thrust him into the international spotlight. In London when the war broke out, he was asked by the U.S. consul to organize the evacuation of 120,000 Americans trapped in Europe. Germany's devastating invasion of Belgium led Hoover to pool his money with several wealthy friends to organize the Committee for the Relief of Belgium. Working without direct government support, Hoover raised millions of dollars for food and medicine to help desperate Belgians. In 1917, after the United States entered the war, President Woodrow Wilson asked Hoover to run the U.S. Food

Administration. Hoover performed quite admirably, guiding the effort to conserve resources and supplies needed for the war and to feed America's European allies. Hoover even became a household name during the war; nearly all Americans knew that the verb "to Hooverize" meant the rationing of household materials. After the armistice treaty was signed in November 1918, officially ending World War I, Wilson appointed Hoover to head the European Relief and Rehabilitation Administration. In this capacity, Hoover channeled 34 million tons of American food, clothing, and supplies to war-torn Europe, aiding people in twenty nations. (Taken from the internet).

We can look back and see the good that came from the enormous struggles the above three encountered. I am sure neither of these felt joyful during the part that they played in history, but for the joy of seeing lives changed, they endured the cross they had to bear.

In the game of checkers one checker can be sacrificed in order for another to jump ahead to be crowned. We are all called to make sacrifices of some type.
If the sacrifice is for the cause of Christ, then joy will come. Joy is our inheritance.

RULE 6
Look to the Rock from which you were hewn (Isaiah 51)

A lying spirit comes to the reasoning of the mind to create from a false image implanted on the mind. When the unrenewed mind consults the Adamic nature of man he opens the door to falsity. Example: Jesus spoke to the disciples telling them that when He leaves to return to the Father, there will be those who will persecute them and even kill them. He told them this so that their sorrow would not overtake them in grief. Under the reasoning of falsity, the mind will try to work out a solution to correct any situation in which that person is feeling rejected or abandoned. "Maybe if I worked harder, they would like me." Or, "If I can only change my appearance, then I would be loved. "These are words which come to the lower nature of man to instill grief and disappointment, often keeping him awake night after night with thoughts that it is his fault things aren't going well. In truth, Jesus tells us not everyone will like us, so let it go and just bless those who hate you and persecute you (I Peter).

Lying spirits speaks to the works of the flesh using the Word to condemn. In John 14 we read:

1. Let not your heart be troubled: ye believe in God, believe also in me.

7. If ye had known me, ye should have known my Father also: and from henceforth ye know him, and have seen him.

12. Verily, verily, I say unto you, He that believeth on me, the works that I do shall he do also; and greater works than these shall he do; because I go unto my Father.

15. If ye love me, keep my commandments.

Jesus told the disciples that He was the truth, the way, and the life. Any question that they might need answered would come by Him and through Him, not by any other source. If they love Him, they would have to keep His commandments. The flesh cannot and will not keep the laws of God.

I knew a friend who walked in the gift of health. She had never been sick once in her life for over fifty years. This woman prayed for the sick and saw them recover because of her faith. She even began to cast out the evil spirits that caused sickness in the lives of others. She was in demand of those needing deliverance. Before she knew it, she was praying for other to such an extent that she forgot to have time to receive from Jesus for herself. The times she used to spend in the Word became less and less until there became a deficit in her faith level. She became a prime target for Satan. I will call this woman Ann.

On one occasion, Ann was asked to deliver a woman from a demonic spirit. This woman turned to Ann and said, (the evil spirit), I am going to kill you. Fear entered Ann. Even though she had been a strong woman of faith for years, Ann could not resist the lie. Ann had spent so much of her time helping others that she neglected spending time with Jesus and building herself up in the Spirit.

Satan sent an attack against Ann in the form of an infection. Ann tried to use her faith to be healed, but with no effect. She was afraid to take medicine, as it would appear that she had lack of faith. Ann became tormented night and day for months keeping her from sleep. Then, at Ann's weakest point, the evil spirit said to her, "you have committed the unpardonable sin, so you might as well kill yourself." Ann listened to the voice and did just that. Ann received the lie by considering "the facts." Ann reasoned in her mind that if she could not get rid of the spirit, she must have committed the unpardonable sin. Ann forgot to consider Jesus that He forgives our sins and restores us. God is a good God. He will not force us to take a stand of "faith" when we are in need of being built up first. I read a report from Dr. Peterson of ORU in Tulsa, Oklahoma concerning a person's immune system. Dr. Peterson found that as we pray in the Spirit, or worship in the Spirit, there is activity that begins in our brain. As we engage in our heavenly language, the brain releases two chemical secretions that are directed into our immune system giving us 35 to 40 % boost to our immune system which promotes healing within our bodies. So, when we neglect the gift of the Holy Spirit, we can become so weakened that disease sets in.

RULE 7
When in the valley of Baca, dig a well.

The name, "Valley of Baca" means a place of weeping. In John 4 Jesus tells His disciples that He needs to go through Samaria. Jesus had to come to a place in which a woman of Samaria would come to draw water.

5. Then cometh he to a city of Samaria, which is called Sychar, near to the parcel of ground that Jacob gave to his son Joseph.

6. Now Jacob's well was there. Jesus therefore, being wearied with his journey, sat thus on the well: and it was about the sixth hour.

7. There cometh a woman of Samaria to draw water: Jesus saith unto her, Give me to drink.

8. (For his disciple were gone away unto

the city to buy meat.)

9.   Then saith the woman of Samaria unto him, How is it that thou, being a Jew, askest drink of me, which am a woman of Samaria? For the Jews have no dealings with the Samaritans.

10.   Jesus answered and said unto her, If thou knewest the gift of God, and who it is that saith to thee, Give me to drink, thou wouldst have asked of him, and he would have given thee living water.

11.   The woman saith unto him, Sir, thou hast nothing to draw with, and the well is deep: from whence then hast thou that living water?

12.   Art thou greater than our father Jacob, which gave us the well, and drank thereof himself, and his children, and his cattle?

13.   Jesus answered and said unto her, Whosoever drinketh of this water shall thirst again:

14.   But whosoever drinketh of the water that I shall give him shall never thirst; but the water that I shall give him shall be in him a well of water springing up into everlasting life.

15.   The woman saith unto him, Sir, give me this water, that I thirst now, neither come hither to draw.

Like the woman at the well, who asked for the living water, we too must come to the well of our salvation and draw out of Jesus what we need. The woman was living with a man who was not her husband. She had five husbands, so her need was great. She was told to seek for whom the Father wanted her to worship. Jesus was presenting Himself as the Messiah. If, in our deepest hurts and longings, seek Jesus, our Messiah, we, too, would find the water to refresh us. This woman has to overcome a religious spirit, the letter of the law, and the feelings of unworthiness. Remember what Jesus said, "I must need go . . . " Jesus has come already. He already went to the cross to meet all of our needs.

RULE 8
The Father looks to restore us to our rightful place.

The Father looks to restore. That which God began in us He will finish. He is looking for all who have left Him so that they might be restored. An example of this is in Luke 15:4-7

4. What man of you, having an hundred sheep, if he loses one of them, doth not leave the ninety and nine in the wilderness, and go after that which is lost, until he find it?

5. And when he hath found it, he layeth it on his shoulders, rejoicing.

6. And when he cometh home, he calleth together his friends and neighbors, saying unto them, Rejoice with me; for I have found my sheep which was lost.

7. I say unto you, that likewise joy shall be in heaven over one sinner that repenteth, more than over ninety and nine just persons, which need no repentance.

God has much to say about restoration. Listed below are just a few verses.

1. Jeremiah 30:17 "For I will restore health unto thee, and I will heal thee of thy wounds, saith the Lord."

2. Deuteronomy 30:3 And I will return and gather thee from all the nations."

3. Hosea 6:2 "In the third day he will raise us up, and we shall live in his sight."

4. Acts 1:6 "Lord, wilt thou at this time restore again the kingdom to Israel?"

5. Psalm 51:12 "restore unto me the joy of thy salvation."

6. Matthew 19:28 "And Jesus said unto them, Verily I say unto you, That ye which have followed me, in the regeneration when the Son of man shall sit in the throne of his glory, ye also shall sit upon twelve thrones, judging the twelve tribes of Israel."

The word restoration means reinstatement, reestablishment, restitution, repair, renewal, and refurbishment. Sin took us to a fallen degenerate state of being, but Jesus turns the tables and restores us back to His original plan for our lives. We might not see it this side of heaven, but we will see it. In the game of checker, once a checker makes it to the other side of the board, he has the legal right to reinstate a "fallen" checker and have it crowned. Romans 8:20-23 says:

20. For the creature was made subject to vanity, not willingly, but by reason of him who hath subjected the same in hope,

21.   Because the creature itself also shall be delivered from the bondage of corruption into the glorious liberty of the children of God.

22.   For we know that the whole creation groaneth and travaileth in pain together unto now.

23.   And not only they, but ourselves also, which have the firstfruits of the Spirit even we ourselves groan within ourselves, waiting for the adoption, to wit, the redemption of our body.

At the time when we will see a partial redemption of something the enemy has had in his control, several things happen as seen in Matthew 21:2:

1.   Jesus begins to give instructions to his disciples for His entrance into Jerusalem (the place where He will be crowned). "Go into the village and bring me an ass and its colt. Tell the owner that the Lord has need of them. The crowning is to fulfill a plan God has for us. We are to humble ourselves under God's plan. The worship of God is necessary for this next place.

2.   Jesus overthrows the money changers.

There are iniquities within us that hinder our kingly anointing that make merchandise of us. We will be called to much prayer. Others will come asking for prayer. We will make judgments after the Spirit's authority.

3.   There will be those who come against the work personally. We will experience the physical or verbal beatings of abuse. Relationships are severed. Rejection felt, the spirit of envy, hatred, jealousy, etc. seen.

4.   Transference of wealth.

The kingdom of God taken from one and given to another who will bring forth fruit for the glory of God.

Acts 3:20-21 And he shall send Jesus Christ, which before was preached unto you: whom the heaven must receive until the times of restitution of all things.

Restitution does not appear until there is a crowning. The crowning brings division. Not everyone appreciates your success. Those who receive you as Jesus and are happy for you receive Jesus. Those who are jealous of you lose the position they once had.

Those who are crowned will soon know those who love them with a pure love.

RULE 9
Pure love

In Philippians 4: Love is the crown that changes a person's life.
1.   Therefore, my brethren, dearly beloved and longed for, my joy and crown, so stand fast in the Lord, my dearly beloved.

2.   I beseech Euodias, and beseech Syntyche, that they be of the same mind in the Lord.

3.   I intreat thee also, true yokefellow, help those women which laboured with me in the gospel.

Both of these women loved God and helped Paul in his ministry, but they seemed to have discord between themselves. Paul urges them to be steadfast in the direction that they have been called to, which is serving God from a pure heart. Offenses between one another causes detours which distract from that goal. The goal being, to be crowned in their work. Discord drains a person's strength and ability to pursue the plans and purposes of God.

Once we set our hands to any work God has called us to, we have to lay aside every hindrance that distracts from a work of love. It was love that gave Jesus strength to withstand the attacks of the enemy. Satan is looking for ways to cause a breach in relationships. Paul was concerned that the lack of unity between these two women would stop the work of the church that was in Philippi.

Love is the crown of life's game on earth. It is not natural to love out of a pure heart. Our hearts are infected by sin and need to be changed into God's love. Paul continues the lessons on love in Philippians 1:

8. For God is my record, how greatly I long after you all in the bowels of Jesus Christ.

9. And this I pray, that your love may abound yet more and more in knowledge and in all judgment;

10. That ye may approve things that are excellent; that ye may be sincere and without offence till the day of Christ;

15. Some indeed preach Christ even of envy and strife; and some also of good will.

16. The one preach Christ of contention, not sincerely, supposing to add affliction to my bonds:

17. But the other of love, knowing that I am set for the defense of the gospel.

RULE 10
Mineral rights

The human body contains certain minerals necessary to maintain good health. When these minerals are lacking, disease attacks the body.

God showed Moses the Land of Milk and Honey that was to be the inheritance of the children of Israel. They were to possess their land. The land we are to possess as our inheritance through Jesus Christ is more than dirt in which a person can build a house upon or farm the soil. The soil contains minerals used to grow a crop and sustain life. When Adam sinned against God, the physical body came under a sentence of death. He lost immortality and received mortality. When we accept Jesus as our savior, our spirit man reverts from mortality to immortality but the physical body remains under the sentence of death and begins to degenerate. Much of the needed minerals needed to sustain the body are lost. Man attempts to restore the structure of the body by taking in vitamins and minerals. These attempts are temporary.

When my husband and I bought 20 acres of land in Reedley, we learned that someone else held the mineral rights. What that meant was, if oil, gold, or some precious substance was discovered, the owner had the right to mine the minerals even if it meant the destruction to the top level of our land.

Satan bought the mineral rights to our bodies due to the fall, but Jesus tells us to "take back" all that was stolen from us, and that includes the components needed to sustain health. It is our job to enforce the restoration of our mineral rights, but this can only be done when we are crowned in the authority of Jesus' name.

The "New Man".

Jesus promises us a "new body" when we are glorified with Him, but that does not mean that we are not to start this process by spiritual warfare on earth by recovering our mineral rights from Satan. Our body is our possession. It belongs to us. Because Jesus was glorified at the resurrection, and Jesus showed the disciples the resurrection of Moses and Elijah at the Mount of Transfiguration, we are to bring down the transfiguration to earth now! To do this involves seeing who we are in Christ and exercising that right to change.

Rule 11
Spiritual Authority

Under the law of spiritual authority, we are to take our position as sons and daughters of Jesus. We were once in bondage to sin and therefore had slave mentality. As a slave, people treated us like slaves. As sons, people were to treat us with respect and honor and not order us as a slave.

"So likewise, ye, when ye shall have done all those things which are commanded you, say, We are unprofitable servants: we have done that which was our duty to do" (Luke 17.9.)

"God, who at sundry times and in divers manners spake in time past unto the fathers by the prophets, Hath in these last days spoken unto us by his Son, whom he hath appointed heir of all things, by whom also he made the worlds;" (Hebrew 1:1-2).

Andrew Murray once said that what the church and individuals have to dread is the inordinate activity of the soul with its power of mind and will. Under the concept of spiritual authority, the spirit of God in man is to rule over the mind and will.

The Spirit of God does not want to kill either the mind or the will, but to bring it to a union with the spirit. In the beginning, Eloheim (God the Father, God the Son, and God the Holy Spirit) created man in their image. Man was to be one with his soul and mind. Eve, then, was taken from Adam's side to become one with him. Adam was not to dominate his wife to make her his slave. They were created to complement each other. Because of the original sin, separation occurred between the soul and will. Women began to be considered as man's servant, not his equal. God, however, continually exalted woman to give her back her position in spiritual authority, not over man, but over sin. In order for this to happen, women would have to have the faith needed to receive her inheritance in Jesus. Men would have to have the faith to see her as the bride of Christ, worthy of honor and respect.

Luke 17 addresses spiritual authority in a parable in which men could relate to, that of ruling over servants.

And the Lord said, If ye had faith as a grain of mustard seed, ye might say unto this sycamine tree, Be thou plucked up by the root, and be thou planted in the sea; and it should obey you.

Jesus is confirming to man that he was given authority over the ground, but it would take faith. He also speaks to men who have servants. They command their slaves to obey him because he has faith that he has authority over them.

However, when it comes to relationships, men were to have respect for women as being the weaker vessel and love them. Love provides, protects, honors, and cares for others. Love does not provoke another to anger. Love remembers how Jesus laid down His rights to be equal with God the Father in order to serve Him. There is no respect of persons with God. He does not see the woman as less value than the man to be bound by a form of slavery. On the other side, He does not see the man as less value than the woman to be bound by her.

"Jesus is the head of the body, the church: who is the beginning, the firstborn from the dead; that in all things he might have the preeminence" (Colossians 1:18). Under spiritual authority both the men and women are to equally serve Jesus, not as slaves, but as joint heirs in the kingdom as the Bride of Christ. Neither is to treat the other with lesser respect than they would Jesus. Jesus "reconciled" both men and women to Himself. Reconciliation signifies "to change thoroughly from," Christians, whether male or female, have been changed from slavery to sonship. Neither is to lord it over one another. Both are equally heirs. This takes faith that Jesus has balanced the books. Women are no longer to be treated as chattel property, but treated as Jesus treats His body.

The opposite of spiritual authority is superstition. Superstition is a false notion or fallacy, something that came to your mind or emotions but which is not based upon the truth in God's word. It is under the spirit of idolatry and whoredom. God will judge all actions according to His righteous judgments (Psalm 9:9-16). Those who put their trust in Him, and not in superstition, will be hidden from the assaults of wickedness and evil doings.

16. The Lord is known by the judgment which he executeth: the wicked is snared in the work of his own hands.

God maintains our right to sit on His throne when we make judgments after His righteousness. Idolatry is trusting in anything other than His righteousness. Paul warns the Colossians in chapter 2:

8. Beware lest any man spoil you through philosophy and vain deceit, after the tradition of men, after the rudiments of the world, and not after Christ.

9. For in him dwelleth all the fulness of the Godhead bodily.

10. And you are complete in him, which is the head of all principalities and powers.

Under the spirit of whoredom (the book of Hosea) a person looks to something or someone to meet their needs to satisfy themselves rather than by God's provision. However, a generation will arise that will seek after the Lord, and from His blessings shall receive righteousness. These, according to Psalm 24, acknowledge that the land is the Lords. He has the right to tell us what to do, yet He gives us a choice as to whether we will seek Him or seek after the spirit of whoredom. If we lift up our spirit, soul, and body to seek after Him, then He gives us the right to rule in His name. This act of humility will be counted for a generation who asks the king of glory to enter his land.

Entitlement: means right, power, and privilege to claim something. Those who humble themselves before God and join themselves to Jesus are entitled to reign in His name. Those who do not chose to believe that they are entitled under a false set of rules concocted by either superstition or idolatry. Entitlement is a gift given to believers but taken captive by wickedness. It is as a checker piece which confronts our movement. Once we see the wickedness of false entitlement, we will have to over-come this vital piece of our land. We cannot confront the spirit of entitlement without our being crowned as having the king's authority to fight authorizing us legal rights as in Esther 9.

Now in the twelfth month, that is, the month Adar, on the thirteenth day of the same, when the king's commandment and his decree drew near to be put in execution, in the day that the enemies of the Jews hoped to have power over them, (though it was turned to the contrary, that the Jews had rule over them that hated them;)

1. The Jews gathered themselves together in their cities throughout all the provinces of the King Ahasuerus, to lay hand on such as sought their hurt: and no man could withstand them; for the fear of them fell upon all people.

2. And all the rulers of the provinces, and the lieutenants, and the deputies, and officers of the king, helped the Jews because the fear of Mordecai fell upon them.

3.   For Mordecai was great in the king's house, and his fame went out throughout all the provinces: for this man Mordecai waxed greater and greater.

4.   Thus the Jews smote all their enemies with the stroke of the sword, and slaughter, and destruction, and did what they would unto those that hated them.

Haman represented wickedness. He sought position and power by the use of lies and falsehood. He hated the Jews and conceived to have them killed. He felt entitled to do this evil because Mordecai would not bow to him. He manipulated the king to sign a decree entitling all the soldiers to kill the Jews. Esther was chosen to reveal this evil plan. The king asked her what he could do for her. Her request was to entitle the Jews to defend themselves. Mordecai was given permission to write a decree entitling the Jews to defend themselves. As a result of the victory, days of feasting and joy were observed.

Esther prepared her heart to ask the king for this entitlement. She also humbled herself before God and honored her uncle Mordecai. As she turned to God for help, He released the victory. A friend of mine, Judy Johnson, shared with me something the Spirit of God gave to her regarding judging which seems appropriate at this time.

Whatever the subject, and in this case "judging", we of necessity have to find the Plumbline of Truth set forth in Scripture, lest we become unbalanced, tossed from one side of persuasion to another. Satan doesn't care which ditch the individual or Church takes. One of his biggest weapons is to take one to one extreme or the other, to just keep one off balance & off center of foundational Truth. In the area of judging & discipline, the Church has been all over the map, some very strictly requiring one to adhere & conform to their standard, while others have removed all, if not most, restraint & forsaken church discipline almost altogether, especially in the name of "love" (only then it often becomes something other than true God-kind of love).

The question now presents itself, as to what Standard the Church is to uphold; who or what Standard is the Plumbline we are to follow? Because this is not clear, the Church has all kinds of standards by which it judges itself, or in this case, judges others.

Many have come to the consensus that since Jesus said in Matthew 7:1, "Judge not, that ye be not judged", we are never to criticize, condemn wrong doing or form opinions as to right or wrong, & God forbid should we even speak these convictions, lest one be labeled as being judgmental.

Satan & the world have successfully utilized this tactic to shut the mouth of the Church & Christians from establishing God's Plumbline upon the earth. Then, as a result, the Church & the Christians have often ceased being salt & light in their sphere of influences, where God has placed them.

The Standard by which we are to align is God's Revelation in His Word, & most often, Jesus is the One who demonstrates that Standard to us, as the very Expression of God's Word (John 1:1; Heb. 1:3).

In Isaiah 33:22, we are reminded that the LORD is our Judge, the LORD is our Lawgiver, the LORD is our King. The LORD is our Standard & Plumbline, for He is a righteous Judge. And of Jesus, in Isaiah 9:6-7, the description given is of the One upon whose shoulders the government will sit, & that judgment & justice will be established, & it is the zeal of the LORD that shall accomplish this.

The problem with Israel is that they had a zeal for God (Rom. 10:1-4), but it was not based on knowledge, nor was it based upon the One who would fulfill these very words in Isaiah 9, because they rejected their "King Jesus" & crucified Him. Paul, ignorant of this knowledge, zealously went about trying to establish this government without a reigning, ruling Messiah, who could shoulder such a task. But we have to remember, Paul was not saved. He was zealous without the knowledge of God. Paul was establishing his own righteousness, but not the righteousness of God.

When on earth, Jesus told us, "Do not judge according to appearance, but judge with righteous judgment" (John 7:24). In other words, we are to judge spiritual things by spiritual standards, not by appearance. And the spiritual standard was God's righteousness.

Jesus said in John 5:30, "I can of Myself do nothing. As I hear, I judge; & My judgment is righteous, because I do not seek My own will but the will of the Father who sent Me." Jesus established the criteria by which we can discern & judge a matter. It must be based upon:

1. Hearing from the Father
2. Not of ourselves
3. The righteous character of the Father
4. The Father's will
5. The mission the Father sent me to do

The purpose & intent of this "Lawgiver, King, Judge" is to "save us," as Isaiah 33:22 says. Our King & Savior, Jesus, came for that purpose (Matt 18:1). "Save" means to make to "feel safe & secure: by helping, delivering, taking vengeance, preserving, defending & saving (OT #3457)." The concept of God as Judge, Lawgiver, King" is not given to us to threaten us with fear of harsh ruler ship, ready to smack its subjects, who dare deviate one iota from its power, but to secure us in the confidence of His Protective Care. This very thing is expressed concerning earthly governments (Rom. 13:13). It is a threat or terror only to those who would disregard its authority by pursuing evil.

Cost of Spiritual Authority

There comes a time in which spiritual authority rises up to confront designated spiritual authority. Zipporah's action was such a case. The Hebrew meaning for Zipporah is beauty, trumpet, and mourning. The Midian name means "a little bird." Zipporah was one of the seven daughters of Jethro who is also called Reuel and Raguel. It was to his home that Moses came when he was fleeing from Egypt after killing an Egyptian for killing a Hebrew.

Moses and Jethro must have become close friends as Jethro gave his daughter Zipporah to him. From this union came two sons, Gershom and Eliezer. Even though Zipporah did not share the spiritual values of Moses, she obeyed the tradition of circumcision even though she was against it at first. Moses, the spiritual leader, failed to obey God in circumcising his son.

As a result, Moses is stricken with a mortal disease. Prior to Moses contact with Jethro, Moses encounters God in the Burning Bush that was not consumed. God speaks to Moses about the cry of the children of Israel and the oppression that they are under. God speaks directly to Moses to return to Egypt and confront Pharaoh to let God's people go.

Exodus 3:12 Certainly I will be with thee; and this shall be a token unto thee, that I have sent thee: When thou hast brought forth the people out of Egypt, ye shall serve God upon this mountain.

3:13 And Moses said unto God, Behold, when I come unto the children of Israel, and shall say unto them, The God of your fathers hath sent me unto you; and they shall say to me, What is his name? what shall I say unto them?

3.14 And God said unto Moses, I AM THAT I AM: and he said, Thus shalt thou say unto the children of Israel, I AM hath sent me unto you.

God has called Moses to be the spiritual authority. There is no doubt in this. But there came a time in which Moses disobeyed God regarding the act of circumcision. Zipporah, confronting death to those she loved, became a spiritual authority by doing what needed to be done. In Exodus 4:24-25 we have this account.

24. And it came to pass by the way in the inn, that the LORD met him, and sought to kill him.

25. Then Zipporah took a sharp stone, and cut off the foreskin of her son, and cast it at his feet, and said, Surely a bloody husband art thou to me.

Some of the references say that both Moses and Zipporah were conscience-stricken over the disobedience, but Moses was too sick to circumcise his son. Zipporah rises up to obey Spiritual Authority—God! The bible doesn't give us much information on the results of this action, only that Moses goes on to Egypt alone. Zipporah's obedience cost her marriage relations for a season. There was a time, though, when Moses meets Jethro, his wife, Zipporah, and his two sons in the wilderness. The Bible says, Moses graciously received them. Nothing more is spoken about Zipporah. I however, see her as a woman who rose up against her own flesh to obey God when she saw that death would be the outcome. This would be her greatest sacrifice, her marriage.

Rule 12
Doctrine of Continuity

The thesaurus defines continuity as permanence, stability, and connection. From Wikipedia it is defined as a principle that "whatever succeeds for the finite, also succeeds for the infinite. The Bible hub defines it as a link substantiated with something previously made. Everything has a beginning, so to find an example of the doctrine of continuity; we must go to the book of Genesis, "In the beginning God created." Once God created something, He spoke its continuance with, "Be fruitful and reproduce;" Or, continue to manifest that which was originally placed into being.

26.   And God said, Let us make man in our image, after our likeness: and let them have dominion over the fish of the sea, and over the fowl of the air, and over the cattle, and over every creeping thing that creepeth upon the earth.

27.   So God created man in his own image, and in the image of God created he him; male and female created he them.

28.   And God blessed them, and God said unto them, Be fruitful, and replenish the earth, and subdue it: and have

dominion over the fish of the sea, and over the fowl of the air, and over every living thing that moveth upon the earth.

The Spirit of God was placed in man. Man was to reproduce after God's image, or His Spirit. There is another law, called the law of motion. An object set in motion will continue to be in motion unless another force causes it to change direction. Once Adam and Eve sinned, the force of death changed the continuance of the image of God. Man would reproduce after the image of man and would stay in that image even if another force entered, the force of the new creation mentioned in 2 Corinthians 5:17.

17. Therefore if any man be in Christ, he is a new creature: old things are passed away, behold, all things are become new.

According to Randy Alcorn from his book "Happiness," on page 140 he states, "Though we undergo change and become new people when we come to Christ, we still remain the same people." This is the doctrine of continuity. Heaven will cleanse us, but it won't extinguish our origin, history, memories, or personality.

Paul tells us in Philippians 1:6 "Being confident of this very thing, that he which hath begun a good work in you will perform it until the day of Jesus Christ." This "work" that is in us is the plans God has for us (I Corinthians 2:11-14).

11. For what man knoweth the things of a man, save the spirit of man which is in him? Even so the things of God knoweth no man, but the Spirit of God.

12. Now we have received, not the spirit of the world, but the spirit which is of God; that we might know the things that are freely given to us of God.

13. Which things also we speak, not in the words which man's wisdom teacheth, but which the Holy Ghost teacheth; comparing spiritual things with spiritual.

14. But the natural man receiveth not the things of the Spirit of God: for they are foolishness unto him: neither can he know them, because they are spiritually discerned.

When God placed His Spirit in Adam, His Spirit continues throughout all generations as long as God exists. Adam's sin brought death to man's flesh, not to the spirit in man. The original sin continues through man until another force, the Blood of Jesus, crucifies it.

In Romans 1:11 Paul says that he finds comfort in the spiritual gift that was placed in man as it will be established at some point in time (whether in this life on earth or the life living in God's presence of eternity). Spiritual gifts and calling are without repentance (Romans 11:29).

That means, that which God placed within man will continue. He will not take them away from us or remove them. When God gives us eternal life because of our receiving Jesus as our Savior, this gift will continue within us until the day of resurrection. God promises to perfect us and perform the work we are called to do. This work, or plan God has for each person, will be completed and credited to our account even if we personally didn't fulfill the plans of God while alive on earth. There will be a time that the righteous will return to earth when Jesus reigns as King of Kings.

Paul makes a judgment against a man living in fornication. He delivered such a person unto Satan for the destruction of the flesh, that the spirit may be saved in the day of the Lord Jesus. The Spirit in man must continue on to salvation even if a person's flesh rebels against God. The flesh does not live under the doctrine of continuity. In fact, the flesh must be crucified. Our spirit and soul lives forever, either with the Lord or with the devil. Both Truth and lies are under the law of continuity. Those who walk in truth seek the Lord and how to please Him. Those who live in a lie seek to please the flesh and deny Christ as Creator. If we continue to seek to please the flesh and deny the Creator, God will turn us over to the vile affections that lead to men desiring men and women desiring women for sexual pleasure, but only for the destruction of his flesh.

This is the original sin which began with Adam and Eve, and there is a chosen sin in which we desire our flesh' satisfaction. Sin opens a door to evil spirits and disease. Not all diseases are a result of our opening a door, but all disease originates from sin.

Rule 13

Books Are Balanced Esther 6:1-10

1. On that night could not the king sleep, and he commanded to bring the book of records of the chronicles, and they were read before the king. 2. And it was found written, that Mordecai had told of Bigthana and Teresh, two of the king's chamberlains, the keepers of the door, who sought to lay hand on the King Ahasuerus. 3. And the king said, What honour and dignity hath been done to Mordecai for this? Then said the king's servants that ministered unto him, There is nothing done for him. 4. And the king said, Who is in the court? Now Haman was come into the outward court of the king's house, to speak unto the king to hang Mordecai on the gallows that he had prepared for him. 5. And the king's servants said unto him, Behold, Haman standeth in the court. And the king said, Let him come in. 6. So Haman came in. And the king said unto him, What shall be done unto the man whom the king whom the king delighteth to honour? Now Haman thought in his heart, to whom would the king delight to do honour more than to myself? 7. And Haman answered the king, For the man whom the king delighteth to honour,

8. Let the royal apparel be brought which the king useth to wear, and the horse that the king rideth upon, and the crown

royal which is set upon his head: 9. And let this apparel and horse be delivered to the hand of one of the king's most noble princes, that they may array the man withal whom the king delighteth to honour, and bring him on horseback through the street of the city, and proclaim before him, Thus shall it be done to the man whom the king delighteth to honour. 10. Then the king said to Haman, "Make haste, and take the apparel and the horse, as thou hast said, and do even so to Mordecai the Jew, that sitteth at the king's gate: let nothing fail of all that thou hast spoken."

Mordecai didn't start out looking for a crown. He humbled himself to serve His God at the place God placed him. Mordecai had gone through much humiliation and abuse, but not unseen by God. At the time when there was to be a change in authority, the books of records will be read and God will balance the books. Like Solomon, our goal is not to be for our glory, but the crown of God's approval as we seek to represent Him by manifesting His presence and character. It is not an act of pride to ask to be crowned with God's wisdom and knowledge and presence. It is our inheritance.

THE WINNING MOVE

Crown Me Joy

Sing for joy to God our strength, shout aloud to the God of Jacob . . . this is a decree for Israel, an ordinance of the God of Jacob. When God went out against Egypt, he established it as a statute for Joseph (Psalm 81:1, 4, 5).

The crown of joy represents a sign of God's deliverance. On May 15, 2016, I was awakened with this scripture. I soon learned that a neighbor of my son and daughter-in-law had died hours earlier. This man had never accepted the Lord in all of his 86 years, and neither had his wife. However, seeds of salvation were sown through prayer, witnessing, and the giving of the Bible to this couple. Knowing that the man was on Hospice and expected to die, my son went to their house and, holding hands with the couple, prayed the sinner's prayer. When I arrived early the morning after this man's death, the wife was radiant with God's presence and exhibiting a crown of joy on her face. God had crowned her with the joy of salvation on the man's deathbed.

The preparations of the heart belong to man. He will choose what he must sacrifice in order to gain the crown. In this case, flesh was the sacrifice so that eternal life could come forth. The crown represents the culmination of man's desires and

God's desires becoming as one. "And round about the throne were four and twenty seats: and upon the seats I saw four and twenty elders sitting, clothed in white raiment; and they had on their heads crowns of gold" (Revelation 4:4). "The four and twenty elders fall down before him that sat on the throne, and worshiped him that liveth for ever and ever, and cast their crowns before the throne, saying, Thou art worthy, O Lord, to receive glory and honour and power: for thou hast created all things, and for thy pleasure they are and were created" (Revelation 4:11).

If we never desire to be crowned and engage in the battlefield against our flesh, we will not have a crown to represent overcoming the enemy. We will have nothing to lie at the feet of Jesus. "And they overcame him by the blood of the Lamb, and by the word of their testimony; and they loved not their lives unto the death" (Revelation 12:11).

Enjoy the game . . . remember . . . we win! Count the war "Joy."

About the Author
Rev. Birdella A. Tucker

Birdella Tucker is a many faceted gift, whom God has given to the Body of Christ. As a pastoral leader with a shepherd's heart, Birdie is open and accessible to those needing help. She not only hears God daily for herself, but readily shares this revelation with others seeking prayer. It is always a ready word, a rhema word that reveals God's heart to His people. As an anointed prophetess, teacher and author, Birdie is a frequently sought after speaker, where she is known for ministering to each person present with a prophetic word from God. As a seasoned intercessor, Birdie also hosts meetings regularly in her home, where she gives opportunity for those present to participate in the discovery and development of their gifts and callings. Birdie has been across the world from California to India to smuggling Bibles into Red China to Israel and back again. She is known by those who are acquainted with her for her unselfish love and devotion to, not only God, but those He has placed under her leadership.